Bourbon-Soaked Thread

SHAY

NEWMAN SPRINGS PUBLISHING
320 Broad Street
Red Bank, NJ 07701

First originally published by Newman Springs Publishing 2021

ISBN 978-1-63692-599-8 (Paperback)
ISBN 978-1-63692-600-1 (Digital)

Printed in the United States of America

To Lilly. Without you, this book would've never happened the way it did. We have had many ups and downs, but I think we're stronger for it. I love you dearly, and I hope you are successful in everything you do.

Drowning yet Burning

The sun burns the tears off my face

Awaiting the feeling I'll never feel of a warm embrace

Driving off the cliff to the deepest end of a piece of lace

Wrapped around my eyes cut by the knife you traced

Soggy lies at the bottom of an unquenchable lake

Drowning yourself with the unfathomable bottle of waste

Challenging your unsolvable case

Of Jack Daniel's you hid from your persuaded taste

Bilingual speaking in tongues and Hebrew

Ring wrapped around the line you drew

Tranquilize the ransom that held you

The strings of denim you pull your spine through

Skinned the animal you angered in me

Carved the blood from 100 proof of Hennessy

Captured her white flag and created a legacy

Promised a dozen roses but held an expensive fee

Caressing the idea of throwing lit cigars on my wood flooring

Numbering the moments I idealized the sound of gasoline pouring

Your face as you realized your imprisonment as the fires roaring

Yet still remorseful eyes intently watching the vultures soaring

Demise of a Saint

Counting stars while covering up your dignity

Movement through shaking glass

Pulling at the faith you faked so easily

Pull the trigger as a rightful task

Conceal the weapon of words you speak, mellow the silence of the gun you keep. Caught in the crossfire of tempting peace like a tiger on a gold studded leash

Crashing into warfare

Morse code as battle wounds

Mouth the words with such thick air

The sun hides the frozen moon

Lost in the conniving thrill of the ride

Sending messages to the God you hide

Your caution sign is on the wrong side

Your befriended demon has left you to cry

Danger reeks around the corner

Filling the streets with hydrofluoric acid

Encaging a sly, sinister foreigner

Attempting to stay placid

Caressing the goblet, tempting the poison. An unsettled soul, you guarded the noise in fighting the idea of an obvious choice when you can't see demise when you're a mistress of poison

She

She listens to the fray and screams she's so high at the top of her lungs she can barely catch her breath to "Wonderwall" or "Here without You"

She dances without knowledge of her every movement in the tan room she hates

She drinks chai tea and dreams of a life out of the cookie-cutter suburbs

She keeps her heart to herself but forces her hand to give it away

She thinks about this one model boy in her building who feeds her christened lies
She describes his every feature like she's reading the Bible, incomprehensible yet beautiful
She wears dragons and tigers on her knuckles, hiding the stick and poke tattoo she will never admit she regrets
She prefers to live out of suitcase because it makes her believe she's never stuck
She so desperately wants to be loved like the movies, but no boy is good enough, but still every boy she meets in an unconventional way is
She has a connection to the serotonin that sad music gives her and the way it moves her
She cries how to save a life and acts it out in her reflection, embarrassed as Mom walks in
She sets goals of a better her but never gets to them because of a lame excuse. She begged her father for a guitar she never tried to learn to play

She gets high to come and get higher by falling onto her bed
dramatically

She kisses her car window to see the imprint of her lips in the fog of
the windows
She draws on the waistband of her jeans and rolls them down to
show her friends, and she loves without reason and hates with
an unfathomable amount of mercy

The Littlest Things

ring pop *for* a diamond

long drive *for* a fancy dinner

cassette tape with our initials *for* a Spotify playlist dedicated to us

movie quote that we imitate *for* a spending limit on a card

glass jar of love notes *for* a Cartier bracelet

"Drive safe, I need you here" *for* a "see you at home"

hot bowl of chicken noodle soup and a kiss *for* a "I don't want to kiss
    you, you're sick"
list of places you want to take me to *for* "I don't know, you pick"

tear shed and a hug, seeing me at my worst *for* screaming at me to
    be happier

guitar lesson with lots of laughter when my small hands can't reach
    the strings *for* never getting around to showing me that one
    note
heel you tried on and unadmittedly felt powerful *for* "I don't wear
    heels, that's for girls"
swear word back and forth with laugher at the end of each line *for* a
    set of sailor speech when you're angry
"Baby, if you have to shave your head so will I" *for* a "Hell no, I'd
    look ugly"

Shadow

Sit on the burning side of the cigarette, dangling your legs over the
flame
Hiding your chest with your arms crossed over one another
As if it makes you look cool and laid back rather than insecure
Down your torso into your pocket lies a broken key to your evicted
home
Oblivious to the idea that you will never go back to your old life
When you know it was never yours in the first place

Silence speaks hymns of a harmony only you can hear screeching at
your ears
Hollow is the shell around your heart claiming to protect it when it's
the most sensitive vessel
A case of green Red Bull you swear gets you through the boisterous
day

Dancing and chasing the girl with a green tie around her wrist and
affinity for danger
Only living for that last insidious breath that you can't hardly wait for
Whisper to the coffee cup filled halfway with bourbon that you're in
love with it

Shaking it around as if it's going to change color or make it taste less
bitter
Holding onto the promise of sleep gripping at your wrists, ready to
pull you under

Acting like you haven't felt the warmth of the blanket you burry
yourself with daily
Dreaming of escaping the thorn without killing the rose in three days
time

Over-the-counter medicine ready to play a game of Russian roulette
with each pill you swallow
Waiting to challenge the cold with heat sweats and shaky fingers and
palms

I hate astrology

Reminiscing through memories while my 2015 Chevy plays the paper kites and old pine. My mind is racing while cars race by on the freeway of the town we both grew up in. It's 11:54 pm and I'm passing your street. I play conversations I dream and dread of having with you next time our eyes meet. The way I look at you makes me hate astrology. Why do I have to be a cancer with loads of emotions and passion? Being born in July is a curse. To exist as an emotional being is like seeing every raindrop as the whole cloud itself. It's not just a drop of water wetting your umbrella. It's an entire storm that festers and mutes the saturation of the whole sky, yet it's beautiful and has an effect that's so vast that it casts lightning bolts throughout the fluffy haze corrupting our view of the sun. it turns into the promise of a rainbow bringing the world a glimpse of color. You're that rainbow to my eyes. The storm will only come when I finally utter those words that sting like ghost pepper seeds on my tongue. I'm simply not sure it will end as beautifully as a storm.

Lace

Eleven months since we have been face-to-face
Ten-minute conversations about work and the weather
Nine reasons I should stay away from you
Eight times I wanted to stay
Seven moments my heart stopped beating
Six rules you broke without remorse
Five songs that remind me of you
Four cards on the table and you played them all
Three personalities living inside of you
Two days of lust that made me stop questioning
One woman's lace I found in your nightstand

Polka-Dot Necktie

Giant souls of his feet but his soul starts to feel defeated

Draped in all the colors of the rainbow but the bowtie around his
    neck suffocates him
Kicking the air as an innocent dance watching them walk by as he
    falls as a bit to laugh at
Selling his personality for a chuckle and a few dollars thrown for
    sympathy with the unsettling truth that he Will never make
    something of himself but a cheap grin

Being spit at and feared by bystanders while their Adam's apple moves
    up and down
Painted-on smile running down his sweat-covered face, concealing
    the acne he developed
A little boy walks by and grasps his Mickey Mouse-esc glove and tugs
    on his blouse
Whispering to him to pick his little body off the ground

He reaches out his little arms and wraps them around his big belly
    and hums happiness
All it took was a warm hug.

You hold the sea in your eyes

Every detail of you was handcrafted carefully by an angel. She took a glance at the lightest level of the ocean and bottled it into your eyes. She poured sunlight over them to make them sparkle like crystals and grew long blonde eyelashes around them to protect them. She knew just how precious they are. She gave them the potency to make my heart melt like the wax of a candle after the flame warms it, and the power to change hue with your sympathies. As you hurt, the marble-looking glass turns a shade of grey that reminds me of haze. That beauty is something I loathe to see, yet find captivating. the pain in your pupils dilates with every tear that falls off your cheekbone. In your brightest of moments, they lighten to a soft cyan that carries the words of love and felicity you speak into existence.
You hold the sea in your eyes.

balancing act

lost in a vast world of forgery and Misinterpretation.

clotting the blood from my left leg as I righteously fell to my knees in sleep deprivation from the world unknown.

I apologetically rise as thoughts ambush my mind without speaking thoughtlessly.

my Psyche swells with anger of the slaughterhouse that we call home

I hold tightly to the family that I was blessed with as we rack our brains to figure out what is making the ticking time bomb of this life tick faster and faster

We are painted clowns in a balancing act of "for your own good" lies and desperately trying to find the truth.

dancing on cinder blocks of those ancient beasts who stomped before us, bewildered by the directions given.

learning to balance on one leg but leaving out the importance of leaning all of your weight on your ankle with full wingspan risen for stability.

as Adam ate the apple blaming it on Eve we blame it on the weaker species due to emotional turmoil.

when those emotions were carefully selected by the only one who knows the truth.

Constantly at war, we leave our morality to the highest of kingdoms dividing us like colored m&m's, carelessly, chambered, and segregated

Our disconnect from reality goes deeper depths than meets the eye as we fall into the abyss of perception and media

Though we all want one simple favor from one another

To find a middle ground on the balance beam

Ellis

As she dances her little fingers across my hand
worries caress my mind
The glimmer in her pupils makes my eyes go blind
The possibility of her tiny waist slipping through my grasp is too
much for my heart
Reminiscing on the days when my life will finally start
Still, I sit there with her feet bouncing up and down her eyes drawn
blank with amazement
As I lift her in the air I realize the roses in her cheeks have perfect
placement
The ruins of probability blow through my hair
As I acknowledge I may have no child to bear
Within a brief moment my world stops and all I see is this small
miracle
Whose whole existence is kindred and lyrical
Every little hair on her head was handwoven by angelic beings
Praying over every strand as her little laugh sings

Captivity

Those who bear beings being forced to conceal their agility while blood is pouring out of them due to the curse of Eve.

While men live lavishly having made more dimes than nickels, our bodies are desperately trying to salvage what's left.

We are only acknowledged when there is a void in need of filling

The false persona of weakness and fragility contrasts against being thrown a bone to keep us at bay like a damn wild horse kept in captivity.

Secretly aware of the damage that a wild creature can catalyze with a single wrong glance.

Forced to tire our hands in the kitchen as they reach for the remote bodying a bellowing seal

Living for everyone but ourselves as we are expected to accept the circumstances given

Born into a world of bidding wars and meat markets over our petite figures

Savagely taking what's believed to be theirs and keeping us in captivity the second we utter our first words.

The last Ash

The faint whispers of the spears digging through his eardrums
The smell of rusty metal and body odor numbing his severed lungs
The taste of blood corroding his white tongue
Accusations tightly wrapped around his neck to be hung
He'd rather forfeit his mortality to actions of himself
Than willingly be pushed off an unbalanced shelf
His actions subsided questioning his mental health
Rendering to the life he received from the cards that were dealt
Getting to pursue your fate of how you resign
From impure thought acquiring a taste for cell made wine
Capturing a glimpse of your poverty line
Committing to self-infliction withstanding the pain of your crime
The ashes drift off of its thin paper seal
As you intently watch the hands of the spinning wheel
If the cries wouldn't stop and the visions were real
Would a burning cigarette be your last meal

Lost unfound

Scattered like the pills she takes
Half asleep and half awake
Tried to run, but no escape
Can't they see it's not her face
Lost in her own mind and she can't rewind
She used to dance in the sunshine
Her voice is as light as a feather
Her chest weighs her down
Unraveling thoughts cling tightly to her
Her conscience is letting her drown
Internal torture has wrecked her
When will she be found?

Silver Spoon

All her hearts desires are graciously obliged
Deleterious words clipped her feathered wings
Her backbone is bruised as feelings were forced to subside
Missing stones in her class ring
Wilting mirage on a rose corsage on an empty wrist
Her burning tears tucked behind her ears summoning a grueling mist
Listening to the lies fed to her on a silver spoon
Caging her fragility shadowing the moon
A dove relinquishing her essence demanding custody of her mind
Born into a contract that she never had the right to sign

Eating Distortion

I hope you understand the havoc you rested on my heart
As if it was a pillow for you to lay your head on carelessly
Your flesh caves into my malnourished ribs feeling of a sharped dart
Skin falling off the bones as my arms fall out of my sweater sleeves
Your words spoke to my bones and put them on ice
Fearing my own growling stomach eating less than mice
Knowing my worth is a figment of my imagination
As I preach to others to love themselves
Hating my weary brain for giving into temptation
Knowing I can't reach, pushing the sugar to the highest shelf
Looking at flesh bunching up
With Diet Pills for breakfast alongside a water cup
The women on screen airbrushed and tightened
I hope one day the scale will lighten

Conceptual art

A work of art dedicated to a life you wish to conspire
Sitting in 18 different uncomfortable positions starting to perspire
A satin robe resting on your silhouette as you carefully rest your arm
    on the easel
Playing calming harmonies that make the moment peaceful
Emulating a feeling of lust through a paintbrush
Envious of seeing the ending causing you to rush
Sweeping across the messages hidden within the page
Bringing forth emotions of happiness, longing, and rage
Giving a provocative glimpse into your mind without giving yourself
    away
Distracting yourself with your favorite excuses you like to say
The mystery in the strokes of your pen waltzing around the border
Thoughtful and corrupted, harshly in order
Without pattern or predictability of what resonates with you alone
Fighting the urge to scroll through your phone
Saying what sets fire to your soul remaining anonymous
With a full willingness to imprint on a timid consciousness

Something blue

When I look at you I see glimmering hope
Airy yet stuffy corset that hugs my body amorously
Drawn to you like a moth to a flame
You light up the night with your glow
Teardrops are dancing as they reflect eternity
Signifying the sheer captivation I'd longed to know
Until death do us part and I hang up this dress
When the veil has been lifted
And we're now sealed with a kiss
Forever together, yet just one night with you
As I pack you away and I glance back at you
A tear rolls down my cheek with unending gratitude
Thank you for being my something blue

Audacity

Knock me down to appear larger than life
The words that you've slain me with cut me deeper than a knife
Paralyzed by your actions masked by wit
Listing my insecurities as a comedy bit
That you tell to your friends to appear butch
Pretending you're a team slapping their toosh
When all I see is a shell of a man
With a balding head and noticeable spray tan
Painting me out to be naive and absentminded
Well that's my last straw the fires ignited

Her every feature

She grew fond of the natural rouge of the apples of her cheeks
The shape of her lips forming two mountain peaks
And the lisp of her mouth concealed under her insecure breath
The softness of her gaze when her eyes didn't see rest
The roundness of her mask blessed her with prolonged youth
Her full lips tickled by a needle gently over her crooked front tooth
Many longed for her beauty though she was unaware
In a sauntered manor she attempts at flattening her thick hair
In rivalry with the hiccup on the bridge of her nose
The vastness of her shadow sets tears from her eyes to her throat
Wishing that her pupils were blue as the morning sky
Dreaming of submerging them in colored dye
Knowing her worth on the inside but letter the exterior vail her sight
Failing to understand the hauntingness of her beauty will never
    weather the fight
Between her racing mind and harmonising intellects,
Learning that appeal of the mind is far more beautiful than the
    appeal of sex

Give pride to the sun

Excuse me for sounding insincere whilst telling you this trope
But the storm I weathered for your sake left me at the end of my rope
You tell me so suddenly without room to cope
With the lesson I learn from your utterance slipping away like soap
I spare no apologies for a fragile figure on a tightrope
Of judgement and accusations you built out of a damaged boat
Guarding your neglect for my passions with a circular mote
Crossing over to a new subject brushing it off your wool coat
Placing a stick between my bicycle spokes
Maniacally lighting your coiled roll of dope
We are not obliged to share the same vote
But at least give pride to the sun for glowing during the smoke

Broken sculptures

A good writer doesn't just write

They picture a thought or an object or a person that grew fondly of

They distilled their thoughts into creative juices flowing through
their psyche

They light the fire in their hearts over and over as the wind blows the
flame away

They haphazardly throw their broken clay sculpture of remarkable
anxieties on a slate of white paper hoping to design something
out of the incoherent letters in front of them

They sip vigorously on the bourbon that fuels their emotions to sky-
dive out of their brains

They carefully analyse and sit with one single line of words wonder-
ing why they try

They die of embarrassment as you learn more about the inside of
their soul hoping to God that you couldn't tell it's about them

A good writer doesn't just write, a good writer shows vulnerability
through their broken sculptures

Rusty Spoon

Sitting at the urban coffee shop I like to call my escape

Drinking from the caffeinated drug steaming in front of me

Fogging up my glasses with my harsh breath

The smell of freshly brewed coffee intoxicating my nostrils with
serotonin

Pure lust of this iron mug clinking against the rusty silver spoon

Stirring up all of my fears of what the next burning sip brings

Not ready to Bloom

Cabernet infused with lies basking in the glow
Foggy recollection my throat is dry yet hollow
I'm not used to this and his touch is effortless
I played hard to get and I lost the bet
My heart forever pays the debt of being swept
I tried to and couldn't possibly refrain
Temptation has grasped me burning in my veins
Trying to bloom caught in the dark without sun
Entranced by jewelry around my body numb
Smoke fills up my lungs so crisply yet seductive
Wrapping my insecurities in your icy embrace
I cling to this moment of closeness and grace
My satin inspired a delicate chase of my lace
Unpredictable and sudden like a storm in June
It was much too soon I wasn't ready to bloom

Summer Wake

You stain like a popsicle on my lips
Hot summer night whiskey breath
Felt so complete lying on your chest
Let me undress your mind and peek inside
Show me all the things you hide
Nobody likes a mirror held in their face
Tell me it's love no not a trace
Dying inside for just a taste
You're the victim bite my bait
You're addictive like nicotine
Set me off like kerosene I'll swallow you whole
Gasping for air you deserve it
Grab your black clothes and some roses
This love is dead guess we earned it

Sweetness

You are sweet
Sweet like Rocky Road ice cream melting on your tongue
Sweet like hot tea with a mountain of sugar on your spoon ready to
    stir into the ceramic cup
Sweet like the smell of a fall scented candle yearning to be lit
Sweet like bruised watermelon falling from your lips with every bite
Sweet like a baby's first laugh that sounds like heaven to your ears
Sweet like a held open door from a stranger
But honey that's just it.
Your just sweet nothing more
I want to validate the kindness that flows through you but not all
    that is good in the world is sweet.
Your warm hands around my waist is just a hug
Your lingering stare is just a glance
Not every moment we share is breathtaking.
It is just sweet

Champagne

You're a bottled up hurricane,
Waiting to pop the cork of an imprisoned world

Unimpressed perfectionist

Decorated in a design that made her palms ache
Perfectly etched sketch of a beaming being
Marigold encrusted jewels wrapped in silk
Careful not to wince or dare to move
Chic or whimsical it entrances her pencil
Thick lines and the soft embrace of fabric
Sheer meticulousness shown on her face
True artistry with a violent cascade
Flowing through a kaleidoscope of visions
Basking in her incandescent work of art
Unimpressed perfectionist eager to restart

The Hatmakers High

Do you know what happened to the men who made hats?

Do you know the trauma they faced?

Can you hear the cries of their static voices?

They can, they did.

Poisoning the walls of their skull with toxicity,

Drawing out their blood from the tip of their needle,

Using every fiber of their materialistic minds, curing the felt to make
    just one presentable
top hat

They feel as if they see Jupiter with the mercurous nitrate distilling
    their brain cells and destroying them one by one
But did they enjoy it?

Did they feel high off of this life inside of the factory reeking of venom
    contaminating their mind until they forget to remember?
Did the hatter really go mad?

Medusa

Slithering snakes ring about her scalp, awaiting her victims' stare
Glaring at time, reminiscing at loss of her gorgeous locks of hair

The hiss from her guard dogs guiding her blind eye to their stealth
    movement becoming cold to kind pupils for her own amusement
Who was once a stunning woman defiant of lust unwilling to throw
    her inflorescence
Her integrity was thrown away at the price of fourpence

Avowed priestess of Athena who was seemingly merciful

Cursed with false accusations to her were purposeful

Affair of homicide to the preciousness of her insides ripped apart like
    soft lavender
Doomed to a forbidden life of miserable ever after

A man of stature and seemingly grace took hold of her right to purity,
    stealing her morals, creating a false sense of prematurity
Sea god of glory and raging incandescence with misogynistic ways
    that blew out the fuse
Unwarranted arrest to the tree sap of Syracuse
Unspoken defeat of an unconsented moan

Created the demon in her that turned men to stone

Honey, I'm Home!

Why is normalcy so damn necessary?

To have a house with a couple babies and a normal life

Soccer practice and slaving over the stove for a "Thanks, Mom."

I mean that's what commercials suggest

Here, have a white clean house with a shiny-tooth husband

Jimmy spilled his sippy cup again, and they make Mr. Perfect out
     to be the helpful husband expecting praise For doing the bare
     minimum of "your job"
To me that's like saying, "Honey, I'm home and I didn't cheat on you
     today," expecting a gold star
And you! You're reading this over a glass of wine agreeing but still
     staying in the same normalcy
And why? You're a wife, it's your job.

Change

What is change?

Couple cents in your pocket ready to be thrown into yet another man's jeans?

New Year's resolution, will you attempt for two weeks if that?

Shiny new boyfriend who's actually good for you so you think it's right for you? "Because he's so nice."
No, it's getting off your ass.

It's keeping up with your workout. not the Kardashians. It's getting rid of negativity once and for all.

Sad truth is you might not change.

You choose.

Spiral

breaking glass, reaching a high note falling so fast, cliffhanger you
    wrote never said how you feel, pricked finger, spinning wheel
a real sleeping beauty, but the devil never sleeps, the edge of your
    sword never cut so deep, conceal your weapon my mind went
    haywire, undefeated army sung in by a choir
all forces rise, we eat like kings tonight

cut out my cold dead heart, phoenix take flight

leave the falling fast to me fill my lungs, watch me breathe, crawling,
    crying on my knees, slit my neck, watch me bleed, leave the
    falling fast to me feel me strain, slip slowly, tornado catching up
    to me breaking ground, tearing trees

Feast

goblet of poison or wine, drink from the Russian roulette of demise
    or divine blood committing arson, smelling of wilted irises and
    bourbon
fanged wolves on the prowl awaiting the tearing of your every organ
    possessed by your charm convicted of witchery
you're gonna pay for the havoc you did to me belt dipped in gold
    notches carved out by lance serpent selling words of romance

the apple of your eye I'm throwing down my gauntlet, sink or swim
    in pool of arrogance
you chew me out while I'm swallowed in doubt, hands on the table
    nerve to call me out fork and knife in each hand

cut me open while I'm damned

speak on my behalf so you'll feel my wrath hope, you're gone tonight,
    you're under attack

join me at the table while I feast at your demise

it's something in this drink while you're stuck inside my eyes, the
    apple of your eye, arrow through your head
are you proud of the horrid words that you said?

gifted arsenic tale of romance

sink or swim in pool of arrogance

sing to my soul, pluck the blackbird's feather, damage my heart. I
    thought you knew better, spoon fed me your lies, but today
    you will die vervain ropes tied to a chair edge of the window
    caught by air

Craters

The moon exhales sounds of purity in love

It softly demands sleepy voices and slowly blinking eyes suggesting to
hold someone a little tighter
Craters holding all of the stress that comes with the sun like pockets
of rest and tranquility

Tattoo

Not just a prick on the skin

Not just a stain on the exterior

But architecture of new meaning

A special memorial beneath layers of your coat
An art form developed within
A tattoo may mark but the message will stick

Easy

scissors run across that red tank top

tee shirt tied into a loose knot

loose like the slut they depict of you

panties on the floor next to his black tar chew teardrop stains down your heavy concealer concealing the nightmare you can never wake up piercing and tattoos making you fear her cigarette butts burning the bottom of the cup men won't like you if you don't respect yourself putting themselves on a higher-shelf Victoria Secret pushing up your dignity

thin lines of coke spelled out in filigree easy
ease into the image written across your head easily removed the stains on your bed tattooed figure, the scars of your victims ripped up tights, heels dark and scuffed stuck inside a pitch-black prism

her sanity slipping away at his thrust

easy

ease into the image written across your head easily removed the panties on your bed, scissors run across that red tank top

tee shirt tied into a loose knot loose like the slut they depict of her traces of chloroform in your liquor challenge a lady, make blood look like wine running up your body to your receding hairline

Are you there little one?

As the sun is rising from its slumber, you tap my shoulder and rock me back and forth
You push your little hands off my ribcage and curiously lean forward
You lift my eyebrow bone to carry my eyelid along with it
I pull you towards my chest and hold you in my arms loosely as my brain starts preparing for the day
You run around to my spine and lean against my back while your tiny feet slip over and over on my cotton sheets
Your little footie pajamas race down to the kitchen and pull the wooden chair to the island
With the bisquick ready for me to stir up
I grab the chocolate chips and cut them open just for you to pour the whole bag in
We share an "uh oh" moment then a faint giggle
We laugh as I chase you around the house as you slip through my palms
I finally catch you
Then I woke up…

Pixie

She smiled without fear of her crooked teeth showing
And laughed so hard her cheekbones were glowing
She dances in circles on the kitchen floor
And clumsily slams into the pantry door
She crafts art out of food and gets her hands dirty
Girls like her are always in a hurry
She finds beauty in the way that the wind moves us
She talks to squirrels and believes in pixie dust
This girl is art and you can tell by her stare
That you can try to tame her but she'll never care

Best Friend

Her long raven hair contrasted the short paper white of mine

Her mind made quick decision as mine took time

Her smile kept me smiling

Her laugh kept me laughing

The raven-haired girl had no fears

Her heart was strong, and her drive even stronger, her positivity magnetic
She is everything I want to be and more

She is my best friend

The Girl with the Lily in Her Hair

What a sweet smile that can melt even the coldest hearts

The strength in her cries tear my heart apart

Sews up her insecurities with a four-point stitch

Every positive word she speaks is motivation at the lips

Her hair is short and purposeful as she walks a straight line to her
　　goals. She wears patterns like a story elegantly trying to be told
I envy her intelligence of the way she treats life like a lemon-flavored
　　cake cut by a thin knife

She listens to music that reminds her of a simpler time

But can have a badass persona that is capable of crime

Still this blue-eyed beauty is kindness and grace

Wearing the lily just above her face

Trouba Chubs

As he's lying next to me with no cares in the world, I can't help but
    wonder what he's thinking about
Maybe rolling around his favorite piece of string or nipping at pincher
    bugs on the ground
Or maybe he feels too chubby, but I love my chubby boy. Is his fur
    too fluffy?
What about his curved nose or his tiny meow?

Is it manly enough?

Does he have insecurities? Is that even a possibility?

I think to myself,

How could something so perfect have a care in the world?

How can a beautiful creature wonderfully made feel such hurt or
    guilt for being themselves. Maybe they don't care.
Maybe I shouldn't.

The Girl of Grace

Her laugh fills these hollow rooms

Like the tattoos fill the spaces of her skin

Though don't let them scare you, she isn't full of gin
Sweet like honey, her eyes only tell truth
The balance of impulse and guilt wrapped in leather
She is as hard as the brick walls I put up

But softer than the sweaters that makes me melt in a second
Even past the tough perimeter, her heart is crazy soft

She makes her arms nice and cozy, like a warm and fuzzy loft

I see the way she admires everyone but her reflection

But her every intention, pure

Pure unlike the same look I see in the mirror
Both admiring each other with deep care

I don't know where I'd be without her raven hair
She has no idea, the impact she's made on me
This girl full of grace

Just add water

In paradise with hair in your eyes
A drink in your hand chilling your thigh
Sugary and spicy it tingles your tongue
Stringy elastic coming undone
Sunshine is blinding and crisping your skin
No care in the world to appear to be thin

This Tan Room

Spread across the walls are too familiar of images
Photographs reminding me of a life I attempt to manifest

A giant picture of a leopard reminding me to be brave or whatever
    the hell I bought it for
And a reflection of the person I strive to be, reminding me of my
    every insecurity
There is crumpled-up papers close enough to my trash can to not
    have to get up and throw it away
Whispering to my desires and failed ideas I can never follow through
    with
In this overcompensating bed I lay on memory foam keeping me
    encapsulated because I'm just too damn Comfortable

I sink into the pile of pillows and slip slowly into a coma of empty La
    Croix cans and broken chip bags
I look across my room to that tan wall. Not close enough to be white
    and clear of distraction and not brown Or black sinking me
    into a darker mindset that makes me thrive at night. Not even a
    cream color that is soft And clears the air I breathe
But tan

Gypsy

Just 2 suitcases and a few grocery bags filled with just the necessities.
Her gas tank half full and her 100's of water bottles as she drives
  around restlessly
One single throw pillow and a thin, compact, little blanket
Ready for a life she's willing to face with
Her hair wild and curly from bathing in the river
Never looking back to the life that he'd give her
She hides out in parks, playsets and trains
Laughing and running free to shelter when it rains
Staying with folks she meets along the way to her unknown destination
She stores a glimmer in her eyes for her next vacation
Though she is never lost and never unsettled
They made her a rose and she tore off the petals
She stole cheetos and lighters from the 76
Ran away laughing and blew the cashier a kiss
With her gypsy eyes and her gypsy heart
The girl with no home was a work of art.

Little Helper

Can you feel her?

The tiny dancer kicking at your brain with every pirouette pointing
her leg so stiffly into the walls of your skull over and over until
your head aches
The pretty little woman counting the scribbles in the fabric of your
mind being roped into them, turning it into a game of hopscotch
Her tiny hands opening the windows to your corneas like a porthole
of a ship awaiting the *Titanic*
Her frail arms rinsing out your eyes with salty water because of the
horrifying images of the world she caught a glimpse of
Her moving the bubbles of ideas to the front of your mind to watch
creativity take place
Her pasting memories of love, lust, and childhood to help you close
your eyes at night
Her fishing for the sides of your mouth hooking and pulling it up to
create a smile to tell others you are kind
Her cuddling up to the softness of your heart and innocently com-
forts it when you share your first kiss with someone that makes
your heart skip a beat
Her riding the butterflies in your stomach 'til you have an uncontrol-
lable giggle as she tickles them
Her waiting by your taste buds ready to indulge in some fine Belgian
chocolate whispering to you to say *mmm*
Her adding insulation to your body when it gets cold as if it's an
inside blanket warming you up
Her playing the strings of your vocal cords as you harmonize your
favorite tune

Her releasing serotonin doves into your whole being, filling you with
 happiness because you saw a fluffy animal or baby
Her drying up your tears when someone you love is gone from your
 sight

Your body is her home as well

Treat her as you feel her.

The Men in Blue

We all fear the men in blue. Weather decorated with badges or just
a black tie

Stepping up those creaky porch steps, holding a file or flag in their
hands

Bad news left in the balance as gray seems to follow wherever they go

These men in their suits, innocent or wise, this is the one thing in
their job they must absolutely despise
The young in the blue, with pants a little too loose and a little too
long, must dread the day that this duty comes along
As fearful and afraid as we are inside the door, I can't imagine having
to ring that dainty little bell
I think of these men in blue and the hurt they must feel

The responsibility of telling a family of the tragedies of their loved
one

Resting on someone who could've been just as close, or someone who
knew nothing

These men in blue, forced to stay stoic in such an emotional moment

Even they break

To the men in blue, as much as it pains me and you, thank you

Shaken Bones

Blue lips and pale face

Shivering body scrawny waist

I'd rather a meal than just a taste

Always defending my own case

Eat a burger, beef up

You are dead with just one paper cut

Twiggy model, show your strut

Gain a figure, you have no butt

Society tells me to love my structure

Chicken legs about to rupture

Social media makes me sure

I am a waste of a feather on a clay sculpture

Concealer around my sleepless eyes

Telling myself starvation lies

"You won't die if you eat two fries"

But run to the bathroom to hurl and cry

White collar wife

Papered nails and a powdered face
He never even noticed her lace
Dinner 5 o'clock every night
Sold away by drapes of white
Cherry red lips and welling eyes
He vowed to her underlining lies
Tight stocking cutting off circulation
Seeing her just as bosomed temptation
Tightening the reigns of his white collar
She fakes a smile as he slips her a silver dollar

Feminin weapon

Watch what you say, she will cut off your tongue
Spit you out like flavorless bubblegum
She plays her cards right in a world of unfit kings
Feeding you liquor so truth serum sings
As the lions sleep she hunts her pray
Calculating her moment as night turns to day
Fatal to the touch with premeditated vengeance
Uses fantasy to her advantage of her intentions
If men can deceive through immature "accidents"
She waits for a moment to feed her ravenous
Let them believe they hold charge of the kingdom
While she curls her hair, she lounges and plays dumb
Summoning the dragon he knows she keeps inside
Will often end in his subtle demise
She does it with class, and a bottle of gin
He soon realised it's her over him

Puppy

He brought me light in a dark time

Gave me company while 'lone

His little form snuggled against my side as I struggle to sleep, little
    blue eyes full of hope and excitement
His energy filling the household

His sweet mannerisms stealing my heart

His loud little barks annoying my little heart

His warm little body against my fairly chilly one

The furry little buddy I will have for life

He brought me light in dark times

Wind and Fire

Starving for chaos and lighting a match to an old building

I have a strong desire right now to commit arson, not to harm any-
one but just feel the warm heat on my face knowing I controlled
something so drastic. Maybe I'll walk into the fire, it only takes a
couple steps

But still not a thought in my head tells me to put it out

I hope there's lots of hay or sagebrush that could make it travel for
miles, but the problem of that is that wind could carry it, and even
though it seems harmless and just sets a cough to the air, a fire is a beast

The beast of an idea of mine

That one decision and one match could let the beast lose

Bang Bang

Like the guns on the TV

Bang bang

Like the drums in the garage

Bang bang

Like your fist on the table

Bang bang

Like the words you shoot at me

Bang bang

Like the holes left in the wall

Bang bang

Like the gun you pointed through me

Bang bang

Like the way they tried to save me

Bang bang

Like the lies that you told them

Bang bang

Like the casket that now holds me

Bang bang

Emerald Soul

The souls of your retinas kept me locked in a blank stare
I'll venture the whole forest with just one little glance
Piece together every little branch to a beautiful woven soul
As I stare between the trees as if the world pauses
And we're the only 2 left
Admiring your image in the perception I perceive
Crafting us out of clouds
You're never gonna understand the tranquility I find
In those emerald eyes I see radiant crystals
Lost in the morning forest with the rising sun lighting my path to you
And even when my vision went color blind
I still had a soul to peek through

Dollhouse

Holding hands through the gates of infidelity

Mirroring the image of a picket-fence family

A dollhouse with walls built on lies instead of trust

A fallen angel guarding savage lust

Vodka starting to taste like water

Violently fighting over son and daughter

They consumed your blood to feed their craving

It is dead, no chance of saving

Puppy Dreams

So cute and so innocent

Little hiccups of baby barks

Racing little toes

The twitch of the ears

The race of the breath

The little yawning wake

The bright eyes to follow

I wonder if humans are like that

Sweet when we dream

With little twitches and mumbles

That aren't laughed at but adored

Do we dream little puppy dreams?

Weighted Blanket

Render me speechless

Control my urge to breathe

Throw me under the clear border

Suffocate my wildest dreams

Leave me with no desire to wake up

Let the water fill my lungs slowly

And wrap me like a security blanket

Kill the music of my vocal cords

Sink me into the frozen abyss

Let the sheerness cascade over my silhouette

Never to return from the arousal of complete consumption

I want to drown

I want to know what it's like

My Hero

My hero doesn't wear a cape
He's definitely saved some lives though
He carried his siblings through tragic times
He's the kindest man that I know
My hero's heart is made of gold
He's hilarious and witty
He would give you the shirt right off his back
He doesn't like the big city
My hero is as strong as steel
To me there's nothing he can't do
If you needed him he's on his way to you
He's fearless and daring yet I still feel safe
My hero is a man that we could never replace
His love for our mother you see in his face
He's after God's will and that he will chase
He's raising my brother you bet he'll be great
My hero is hardworking and never complains
He's got the answers and he fills in the blanks
Did I tell you my hero's in his jobs hall of fame?
My hero is my father if you still haven't guessed
When I tell you I mean it he's not like the rest

Yellow

What if the skies were purple during the day
What if the sun shined a shade of green
What if kindness was a person who has held your hand and alcohol
    was spiked with glitter
What if a stop sign was a "get out of your car and dance" sign. What
    if dancing was how we expressed love
What if people were the colors we are feeling in that moment, would
    you be my yellow

Twenty Something

You hand me the candy coated morsel
Careful not to crack it or crumple it
I open it and when I do I see nothing
There is no decadent indulgence inside
Just the wrapper
Now you are grown and you laugh because what you didn't know was
it was never about the desserts it was about that shiny wrapper
that got you to the delicious chocolate you waited so long to
indulge in

Just Flow

Appreciate the air smelling of the town bakery

Appreciate the sound of children playing as you pass the park

Appreciate the taste of Mom's chicken she burnt a little but worked
hard for
Appreciate the feeling of regret after your first breakup
Appreciate the heart you had to give away for it to come back maimed

Appreciate the kindness you felt by a stranger's smile on the road

Appreciate the love that is shared between two people sharing a
milkshake

Appreciate the bliss of driving in the rain listening to cozy songs

Appreciate the connection you feel when your dog looks at you with
pouty eyes

Appreciate the rocks on the ground that give you traction in the river

Appreciate the trail of hearts you changed just by a simple word or
two

Appreciate the fondness of yummy foods you have thanking your
tastebuds

Appreciate the wall that's up to guard your most important organ

Appreciate your eyes to see

your mouth to taste

your ears to hear

your nose to smell

your hands to feel

your arms to move

your legs to walk

your ribs to guard your heart

Murky

We started out colorful
And now the waters gray
The first to fade was yellow there isn't sunshine on our face
We tried to mix in green and white to try and stay afloat
It all turned blue and me and you are stuck crafting a boat
I pinch your skin it's pink again some color has come back
The saddest of all colors the deepest darkest black
When I think of you I see red not blue. You really heat me up
Like a crumpled purple shirt I'll never hang you up
An orange jack o lantern carved kiss anything to dismiss a night of
    grueling loneliness
Grab a canvas and start with another blank
Oh wait we just ran out of paint

Demolishing my fairy tale

A little girl with eyes of redwood and honey
Sitting with a book and her little pink bunny
Reading tales with a prince and a crown
Bubbly dresses and lacey white gowns
Singing about chores and baking raspberry pies
Talking birds and little mouse spies
She met a boy and her little heart froze.
They danced around the playground as he picked her a rose
She ran away frightened as he pushed her on the gravel
Her parents laughed as they watched it unravel
She's grown an inch or two as he grew four
They played basketball and never kept score
He took her to the movies in his brand new car
Stole bourbon and whiskey from his daddy's bar
He wore a black tie and she wore a sheer vale
They rescued a mutt with a cream colored tail
He worked till he was blue in the face
She never really wanted her space
They started to fight, he started to lie
The laughter faded and she ran away to cry
He went out one night and never showed up
As she downed another vodka 7up
She fell asleep and he tripped in drunkenly
Waking her up from the perfume of his company
They screamed, he begged, nothing was left unsaid
With a cracky voice she whispered "our love is dead"
He fell to the ground and wanted to bail.
As she said softly "thank you for demolishing my fairy tale".

Satin Ribbon

Cutting off circulation of my blood making it apparent that my veins
are real

Confiding in the mere thought of forgiveness of the skin barrier that
breaks

Appealing to the idea that it feels pain of a thousand symphonies in
one's ear

Still clasping back as if it's a rubber-banded boomerang that hits with
false pretense

Collecting the stars I see as if I am a cartoon rabbit hitting their head
on a wooden board

Watching as the exterior becomes a shade of blush that Sephora won't
sell

Blindfolding my pupils with a single salty tear caressing my outer
cheek

Bleeding pheromones of a monster I like to consider a torturous
friend

Dressed in satin tied with a ribbon sealed by twirling it with scissors

I gotta be honest

I gotta be honest you've captured my soul
You grabbed a hold of me like I was your goal
One night was all I needed to feel defeat
I gave you a life sentence the night you met me
Inseparable even if we were ever apart
Intriguing just like a genuine work of art
I found tranquility when I surrendered my heart
You caressed me and kissed every one of my scars
In you I found all that I was searching for
I'm so grateful to you for never shutting the door
All that we have is all I was searching for

72 Degrees

It's 72 degrees. Can we turn up the heat?
Covered in blankets, but not wanting to sleep
I reach for your hand, but I don't make a peep
It's quiet tonight, will that last do you think?
Any sudden movement will cause a quake
They have no knowledge of what's at stake
Please come closer, I've got a chill
Not asking for much, not even a thrill
I'll say it again and again on repeat
It's 72 degrees damn it turn up the heat!

Cinder Blocks

Balancing above by head signed with deep red ink

Fleeing from my psyche rendering my skin pink

Flesh decided to melt of the bones that hold me tight

Drawing me out of my shell during a sleepless night

Caring for me as a brother yet holding me hostile

Ingraining the filigree into an ancient fossil

Content with my posture and the message that can fall

Tearing down the architecture of a cathedral wall

How does she do it

She wakes up at 4:30 a.m. to make breakfast
She rests 3 vitamins on her tongue with a large sip of water
From her clear as mountain air water bottle
Her eggs gently crack onto the nonstick pan as she adds all the greens
    from her garden
Her blender is rustling about with oats and homemade powder
She slips on her leggings one leg at a time and slides into her clean
    shoes
She runs without a drop of sweat on her browbone
And her hair perfectly intact as she folds down her yoga mat and
    meditates to rain
She begins writing out her day in a black little notebook
She sits with her coffee as I walk into the room
I am still in my robe and a knot in my hair
I fall on the couch and reach for the remote
Finding anything to occupy my brain as it awakens
I pop a waffle in the toaster and set it on a napkin
She rushes to find her bag and walks out the door
With a voice far too peppy for my ears
I glance at her wondering,
How does she do it?
Well she battles with salads, and the number on the scale
She challenges her body to go without three meals a day
She fights with her lover as he robs her of her worth
And she craves the feeling of fitting in a size zero
She doesn't see that she's enough
She's prom queen, it girl, has it all together
Yet her insecurities flood her eyes as she refuses to wipe them away
She's just a girl constantly trying to be simply good enough
How does she do it?

Machine, Machine

Stitch on straight little double railroad lines

Where little buzzing bees come to life

Put together those two little fabrics

Make a masterpiece of those sheets

By hand it takes a lifetime

While your being saves time

Oh little electric robot plugged into the wall

You are a little lifesaver to us all

Sungazing

We were taught that blindness comes from staring into the ball of
    fire in the sky
Yet we challenge ourselves to glare long and hard as it contrasts
    against our eyes
It burns us to the point of tears and we quickly look away in defeat
But satisfied that we rejected the rules of the elite

Label Maker

She's not the type to just give in and she despises bets she loses
If asked her favorite item in her home, the label maker she chooses
She wants to let the voices quiet of telling her enough is enough
She questions all the time the items she had just given up
To them they see freedom and relief no care to cling to necessities
They don't see the sadness as she squeezes into her jeans
Another denim tossed aside a tear creates its home
They look at her possession less as if she's sitting on a thrown
Queen of being unattached
Is that the road she roams alone?

Liar

I try not to think it but your intoxication is too strong

I don't know how to comprehend you

I kind of sorta want you

And your debonair charm and use of "I'm sorry"

You are trying so desperately to be yourself you forgot how to act
     around me. I'm the mistress of your lies
Saving your rep considering me to be the ruthless temptress, but the
     intoxication of your eyes alone
Just make the drum in my heart to pound so fast as if I'm having a
     heart attack. The smell of pinot noir still makes my hands numb
I catch myself smiling at the wall at night feeling you there

The songs I sing are always connected to a feature of your mind

And the lies you made me tell just to impress you

Can't help but wonder who's on the right side here

The manipulation was so pure like your favorite liquor

Your toxicity drives me down a road of forgiveness and self-abuse I
     don't know what I did to deserve you

Fabric of Time

Taking thin steps to the room I used to know
I reminisce on the clutter that used to grow
Glancing at the mirror and the messages I wrote
Body image and self love notes
Directing my eyes to my purple bed frame
Carving of my first and their last names.
Followed by stickers by Lisa Frank
And an empty foggy fish tank
I flip through my closet like a colorful book
And shimmied on the shirt that hung on a blue hook
Stretching the fabric of time in a stitch
Ripping the seam to a hole that's an inch
Gasping as my body has expanded
My wish for C cups was finally granted
I giggle and appreciate the size I became
And how I used to cry because of my wide frame
I found love in my silhouette and all that it does
Feeling so blessed to have changed from the girl I was

Contract

signed on the dotted line so blindly

naïve and vulnerable, to the roped you held tightly Indian burns and
    no circulation
i wish i never gave in to your temptation

blood edged into your fingertips printing the page from that night
    my cheek got in your way
my vision so blurry like ripped contacts making me sign Lucifer's
    contract knuckles print blood

punching the wall

tears flood

eighty missed phone calls

i'm sorry, baby, come back to me

cut my hand, it has a heart beat

edged into my memory like a folk song

"my sweet, my babe, my love i was wrong"

Fallen Embers

Her warmth I was content with
It was comforting and familiar
A new age I was becoming
I would wait for her to get here
If I asked her she'd say I cannot stay too long
There's going to be a time when this day will be gone
So until that morning comes where there's no heat starting early in
    my day
I'll cling to her until October steals my joy away
There isn't comfort in crisp weather
Cardigans I don't enjoy
As I watch the fallen embers and say my sweet goodbye annoyed
I look forward to many months from now as heat will again fill up
    the sky

Famine

angel craving chaos
devil seeking peace

hellfire holy water
crawling on my knees

we drink the poison our mind pours for us captivated by sex and
    bloodlust
casted into the world unknown

covered by lethal moans
angel craving chaos

devil seeking peace
hellfire holy water
crawling on my knees

tie my body to a plank
chastise me 'til my mind is blank

my heart at bay, my hands at rest
you fall near and soften my chest

silhouettes dancing in the night
the poetry our lips write

we drink the poison our mind pours for us captivated by sex and
    bloodlust
casted into the world unknown

covered by lethal moans
angel craving chaos

devil seeking peace
hellfire holy water
crawling on my knees

power of free will at my fingertips, testing thoughts of danger tasting
its lips, calling the mountains to shake when i call casting my
fears of my highest fall, balancing act of time and death

'til my soul is put to rest
angel craving chaos

devil seeking peace
hellfire holy water
crawling on my knees

Silk Pajamas

I wish to be that woman in the silk pajamas you see in movies
But Is this what they want from me?
A mundane life with a simple job
A beautiful family to go home to at the end of the day
A husband who cooks you dinner and opens your beer
A concert in your shower as the hot water runs down your chest
A visit to grandmas with three carseats in your Ford Fusion.
A Sears christmas card addressed to your loved ones
An oversized cotton pajama set as you cook pancakes in the morning
But what if I also want...
A crowd of those who enjoy my work rushing to catch a shot of me
     in public
A script in my palms as I analyze it over and over
A met gala ball gown that drapes to the floor crowded by diamonds
A dinner at a restaurant with a menu that lacks prices
A set family made of creative souls that I get the opportunity to share
     a screen with
A position of power to change the way the world views women
A love for every form of art that I get to share with the world
A set of silk pajamas grazing my perfectly shaved legs as I stare heavily
     thankful for the life I created for myself
I will get my silk pajamas.

Blood Lust and Angel Dust

She finds herself at the bottom of a deep and dark abyss

Collecting bodies of water to stay hydrated within her chapped lips

Casted out of a place you could call an angelic battleground

Of love and lust fighting for triumph to be found

Considering flames of ice defying all odds

Falling for impurity as he casts out his rod

A black figure with a reddish hue

Is saving face by so-called "rescuing you."

Shrunken dress

I look at you in disbelief that you came from me, so little and sweet
You squirm around as I put on your dress, I hold your frail body, you
    warm my chest
Your giggle is sunshine, lips locked on your pacifier
As it falls from your mouth your scream gets higher
You take your first steps and catch yourself with your tiny hands
You tug on my shirt for whipped cream and teddy grams
I open my bag that I never hid away
Filled with things I took to the hospital that day
I pulled out the things that were once in my hope chest
Including what you came home in, the little flowered dress
And overnight, you grew like a daisy
Running around the house like crazy
You rustle through my drawers and make a mess
Shouting "mama, I shrunk my dress".

Cough Drop

Here take a cough drop she exclaims
No thank you I smile, but she can't refrain
My throat doesn't hurt and I have no pain
Why on earth do I need a cough drop
It's too late she grabbed it out of her purse
She put it in my hand like it's been rehearsed
Demanding I take it and not backing down
I tried to be polite and she's starting to frown
Exhausted from the back and forth
Tired of being stubborn
If I hear the word cough drop one more time she better run for cover
I grab it frustrated and swallow my pride
I gag at the flavor, but it's cooling inside
I crunch it up quickly so it doesn't last
She rolls her eyes at me and says that was fast
No matter what I do she'll never be pleased
Women like her think rebellion is a disease

Sister

She laughs without fear of sounding too bold

She cries like no one is watching

She lives in a world of pink Moscato and '90s shows

She drives an old beat-up Chevy always on E

Her heart is worth far more than gold and rubies

Her selflessness toward every little creature

Her way of talking is far from gentle but unassuming

Her hope for children with her every feature

She feels like summer with the sunflowers blooming

She speaks words of wisdom without putting them into action

She catches frogs and lizards with her whimsical eyes

She has over a million passions

Her arms tightly wrapped around me when I cry

Her soft insecure singing voice

Her never wanting to say goodbye

Her love was never a choice

Manipulate Me

I am completely compelled by your spirit and the way you hold my
    heart
With your calloused hands wrapped around it like a pillowcase
Your eyes are kind but have deeper vengeance
The layers of my mind are torn apart one by one

I cannot fathom your mendacious tendencies that whisper "La vie
    en rose"

Trying to explain you is like trying to explain death

Unsettling yet undeniably beautiful

Empty battery

Crowding around me as my eyes go fuzzy
I'm trying to speak but my air is muggy
30 sirens shooting off their mouths fast pace
I'm dreaming about running to home base
I start to feel dizzy as they all speak at once
My head is a football they can throw and punt
My face relaxed as I blankly stare
Their laughing and whispering but I can't see them there
I sip my rosé and nod as if I understand
While all my attention goes to 1000 talking hands
I sit on an air vent in the room with no one to talk to
As my social battery empties and my lips turn blue
I hear the loud vocals even over the fan
I mask them by covering my ears with my hands
I lay on the floor as my social battery gets lower
My words become slurred and my thoughts become slower
My tank is on empty and batteries dead
Just let me lay here and rest my heavy head

Pastry Chef

Alone in his kitchen he designs a marvelous cake
He baked it and frosted it now he's barely awake
The career he chose is indeed a special sweet treat
There's just one problem he's missing his ethereal peach
Sweet and savory she had it all
He can wait an eternity sadly she'll never call
So he distracts himself with truffles and cakes
And if they dare notice him tear up he shoves flour on his face
When she left him too soon he knew he'd never be the same
So he moved out of town and made a new name
Ironically the cake he just made is for an anniversary and the date it's
    the same
As he decorates it with peaches he
Feels a cool breeze it's whispering I love you and it caused him to freeze
He looks around, but he doesn't see her
As he boxes the cake up he's thankful that possibly she's near
He cracks a smile and thinks to himself what a tough year
I love you he cries as his eye drops a tear
How he wished she was here

Heaven Concealed

Sending messages from above

Hiding from me but still with the ones I love

Graciously calling out my name

Idolizing air and declaring her fame

Reaching for stars as the sun is setting

Catching a glimpse of the moon and cloud's wedding

Detailing every feature of his porous face

Hiding the clouds with pillowy sheer lace

Pulling at the strings of the mesmerizing harp

Cutting the notes in half with an A-sharp

Holding the carousel of faith for ransom

Calligraphy to the eyes hopeless to fathom

Volcanic ash turned to streets paved with gold

Ruptured reality tantalizing my soul

Ingrained in omen forged in doubt

Clear directions but took the wrong route

Nerve of a siren singing in Hebrew

Pulling you out from the God that you knew

Nulliparous

A dire decision made a long time ago
Delaying, but wistful she's ready to know
Herbal healing adds warmth to her home
Paving a foundation she's anxious to sow
Convincing herself it won't be like before
She clings to a layette and closes the drawer
Fearing her future will slip through like sand
Crumbling her paper they don't understand
Tears and begrudging feelings pour out
Suffocating slowly she chokes on her doubt
Frantic to flee her dismal reality
And return to the woman she's proud to be
Her body is worn out and her insomnia grows
Feeling betrayed by a thing she never chose
Anger creeps up on her and hardens her bones
Praying this grief doesn't swallow her whole
Pinching her flesh causes her to wince
Pleading, but no use trying to convince
Immediately there's a heated stinging relief
Finding comfort in the burn it's only temporary

Bird Boy

The wilderness was tangled within his auburn hair
With a devious smile and emerald green eyes
He dreamt of a life beyond the border of a birdcage
Forced to sing so he chose to die.

The Sorry I Don't Mean

The urge to apologize creeps up my throat

The intentions of your stare make me ponder if this is just your world

The innocence of your small breaths making me weary of your sincerity

I graciously and cautiously speak false hymns of nothing

Regretting instantly the forgiveness of the audacity you had

Being polite will keep you out of trouble, sure?

But it's become a habit of insincerity and manipulation

Taught to little girls since we were old enough to speak

So, no, Brad or Ryan, I'm not sorry!

I probably had a damn good reason for doing what I did

But here, for your overcompensating ego

Here's the sorry I don't mean

A mother's way with love

Not so gentle
Not so charming
Her artistic ability is kind of alarming
A woman of condensed sugar and burn your nose spice
She kept it together and refused to play nice
She was stubborn as a mule and as so was her father
If you wake her up too soon don't even bother
Though a heart of him too, soft as a teddy bear
Makes a perfect home in her heart, pillowed with prayer
With a little bit of dits and a gigantic smile
She lived for her loved ones and would drive a million miles
The woman is a gun who refuses to aim wrong
You ask to sing for her and she'll clap for every song
Not so quiet
Very exceptional
mama you are absolutely unforgettable

Clay Figure

Perfect position and potent posture

Scarce calls of nonexistent ambitions

Perfect shape and unapologetic size

Earsplitting whispers of low self-esteem

Perfect rhythm of an unconscious fight

Reeking stench of unworthiness

Perfect stealth of ignoring the sniper of love
Disruption calls of depression knocking
Perfect imprisonment of the light word relationship
Deep, weary screams of failure to commit perfection of the mirror
    worsened

The harsh reality of the never changing

Clay figure

Carry me Higher

Its 3:28 a.m. and I'm falling down a rabbit hole of wonder and terror
all at once
Her branches tickle my shoulder blade like a lively feather fallen off
a peacock
I chose at random the next leafy rope to climb as she calmly pushes
my bottom upwards.
Leading me to the top of her mountainesque peak petting my fluffy
hair with the wind.
I call to the horizon in a harmonic ballad wishing I could stay here
forever
The clouds rush to me as the wind blows me upward
I'm consumed by the marshmallows and fluffy white smoke
He whispers to me to glance at the earth, waving at strangers and
watching the cars go by
The wind blows me away back to the tree who was always there to
catch me
She hugged me tight and I thanked her softly as I drifted away
Back to my cleat mark on the ground where the pages of my book
ran wild
She caressed my chin and fell back into place, where her branches lay
purposefully
My eyes pulse open and I glance at my story
That carried me to new heights

Draining the bottles

Pounding headache throbbing my skull
Light stinging my eyes
Clinging to the sink as my stomach turns
Stupid girl you never learn
Tequila wasn't my friend last night
Rum wasn't my lover
Nowhere to hide so the toilet I hover
Slow-burning crawls up my throat
Sinking into dizziness desperate to stay afloat
Looking in the mirror I don't see the same eyes
They appear bleak and not blue inside
I crawl into bed and pull the covers over me
If I sleep this off maybe I'll be fine
That's the final straw I'm draining the bottles

Traffic

Cruising around at a steady pace

Keeping me in the right gear

Taking nearly endless stops until I am seconds from oblivion, reaching new levels of tranquility of madness as I rush to go turning corners recklessly and speeding into new lanes without regard, blurring out signal and neon street signs on full volume I muted, spinning out into a concrete capsule of invisibility

Counting the moments before my mind divides itself like the white lines stuck in a plethora of vehicles awaiting the green light
Lights flashing giving me screeches of absence

barking at me like a blinded guard dog to continue through but still get bitten following directions with a bone chilling urge in my body
Keeping my eyes on the passenger seat as if it's a helpless version of myself in spirit tied down with a seatbelt
Naive to the bloodshed squirting out from my veins. Should have seen the car coming

Airy temptation

We know the dangers the thick smoke brings
Yet we still breathe in deeply
At least one gasp of fatal air.

No stranger to serpents

My nerves spiral down my spine like a slide into my past
As a snake appears out of smoggy thick ash
I quiver and hide as he grabs me by the throat and captivates my eyes
Letting him know I'm reading his premeditated lies
He may be tempting and charming as hell
But I have met him in other forms, I know him quite well

Caramel Apple

I want to inhale you like a supple flower
Never forgetting your honeyed aroma
I want to clutch your heart in my hands
I know it's fragile and can break
I want to savor the caramel on your lips
Intoxicate my mind with your satire
I want to devour your anterior
And grip onto your delusion
I want to scrutinize every detail of your being
Share your somber confessions
I want to dive into the deep end
Give me the keys and let me in
You're sour like an apple
I'm trying to bust down the walls
Open up your chest
Or I will start a war

Aries

She's mine and she knows it
She's assertive and owns it
She's dark and obsessive
She's clingy and aggressive
She craves my warmth
She's not italicized she's written in bold
She's a fire sign so be careful not to get burnt
She's in control of the seasons
She keeps me alive inside
She's learning lessons the hard way
She's confident and she will make you her prey
She's first in line to the zodiac thrown
She's ruled by Mars, she calls it home

One Little Bite

Hi just checking in, beautiful.

How are you?

Have you eaten today?

It's okay if you haven't, but can you do me a little favor?

Can you grab something you used to love out from your pantry right
    now? Just hold it in your palm and sit with it.

Toss it in the air

Rock it back and forth

Now take however much time you need to unwrap it or cut it up

And close your eyes

Are they closed?

Now whenever you are ready take one single bite

Just one little taste of whatever used to make you smile
Now take one more if you can
Sit with it for five minutes if you have to
Drink a sip of water with it.
Now it is your choice to eat it all but for me

Would you eat just half?

It's okay if you have not

It's okay to not want to

Sweetheart, it's even okay to feel sick at first, but just eat half, or even
  a quarter
I am so proud of you either way.

Have you eaten today?

Mr. Monday

He feels like Monday with a dash of depression
His oversized coffee cup and messily parted hair
Right down the middle thinking, he's some 90s actor
He keeps a little black book of all the area codes he collects
Distracting himself from his sleepy eyes
With a briefcase filled with possibly pressed documents
Or maybe he's a dealer and it's full of paraphernalia
Or it's made up of nothing but a cliff bar and a few post-its
Is he trying to prove himself?
Make a statement and prove himself with an empty briefcase?
Or is he simply headed to work?

Wicker Basket

Woven like our hands were

You hold blankets like he held me

A warmth you bring into the world

Lighting up a room with your little woven handles

Overflow with the love we shared

Until your woven handles broke

Our hands left each other

Your presence got cold

And your basket became empty

Tiger Eyes

Wears pelts of gold and black velvet wrapped around his sickly figure
    compelling you with his magnetic demeanor
His hot potent breath mythically whispers to your psyche to lie

Warning your fingers not to meet yet pulling your waist in as if you
    are one single pound with an unreliable amount of force
Taking the souls of your feet glued to the heels he buckled you into
    with hidden needles in the vamp of the stiletto you already
    could barely walk in
Pressuring time to turn into a saber to wound you with drunkenly

Wailing the sounds of emasculation as his loyalty slips away stealthy
Demonic murmurs emitting from his yellowish condescending
    pupils

Finding your weakest vessel of your heart feeding on its compassion
    for the broken
Using catlike reflexes to dim your sight for him to prey on you
Many see eyes of honey glass and a charming smile
But the tiger in his eyes sees you as a slab of flesh on a skewer
Readily awaiting to tear it and feast on its naiveness

811

Bleeding out from my heart on to the poetry I drew in my skin

Not 911 what's your emergency?

I couldn't call it that

Not good enough of a story for 911 to rush to my aid

Not as simple as needing a flashing red chariot coming to my rescue
I'm not a damsel in distress
Not an emergency of needing assistance

I'm fine, I know it

811

I'm not good enough for 911

Not even close

911 is for a car accident or heart attack and my heart is definitely
    under attack still no need for relief

I'm fine, I know it

I am

"911, what's your emergency?"

"Hello?"

Give it a Rest

I just sat down and low and behold
He noticed my drink and my lack of a coat
Here comes the tattooed man who thinks he is bold
As if a glance was an invitation to stay next to me for a while
I feel goosebumps creep up on my skin
He thinks my cheeks turned red because of him
Don't humor yourself it's the cocktail I downed
I forgot how to think with you breathing next to me.
I came here to dance and eat and I can't do that with you bothering me
Just because I'm alone doesn't mean I came here in hopes we'd stum-
     ble back to your home
I don't owe you my digits please don't touch my phone
You've just crossed the line, but the alcohol makes it fine, right?
You're rambling on about everything that gets you in the mood
Can I cut you off? I don't mean to intrude
I'm going to be honest I think that you're small
The fact that you want me to grab it says it all
That tattoo you got that's still not done
Already told you we'd never have fun
See I'm a cancer. I enjoy the romance
I lost all hope when you didn't ask me to dance
And before you get up yes I'm demanding you leave
My vertical smile wasn't yours to try to achieve

Runaway

I want to run. It's all happening way too sudden like the drop of a rollercoaster with too much anticipation for my heart to handle. New places are good. I want to run to a quiet place to fall as if I was that saying, "if a tree falls in the forest would you hear it?" or something close to that. I hope when I fall no one is there to help me up or tell me it's okay. Just to fall. Let my head weigh 500 lbs and tumble me forward into nothingness. I don't want to grow wings or land on pillowy leaves. I want to fall than start running again after trial and error. If I just keep running, I'll make it to nowhere where I long to be. I'll find shelter but never a home. Home is too safe, secure, loving. I want to trip and I want my palms to blister and my knee caps to collect dry blood to feel the pain of having nothing to heal you. I want to leave the place where comfort swaddles you like a newborn. I'll find a new tree to fall from here and there, but just to be a runaway... I'd give anything

Jester with a Rusted Crown

Acid rain into the flask he drowned you with

Controlling your walk holding you by the hips

Stealing kisses off your bruising lips

Charming you with his bag of tricks

Swallow the bottle, feel a burn in your chest

Does it sting like the metal he edged in your breast
Empty promises of a full nest
And with the blood gushing from the knife that gave you rest
Now who is the babbling fool?
Put him on a golden pedestal

Now he's a jester, naive thinking he rules

Your heart and his blade was an unfair duel

A cheap laugh was all he had to give to you

Watching you freeze to death as your lips turned blue

Slipping through the cracks of undeniable doom

Yet you thought he could save you?

Rain

If you look closely, it's not plastic, it's glass

Shiny yet fragile, convincing yourself it will last

But it slowly will fade like the faint trickles of rain

Dripping on to your windowpane

Another night he's called you insane

Another day of wishing you stayed away

Time, can't it just fade?

This is a false forever and you know it yet

Your faith consumes you of the storm you both weather

I Can't Believe It's 5:00 AM

I'm sitting here writing whatever I attempt to feed my ego with bit-
ing my lips so hard they bleed as I use that as a thinking method
reminiscing on every sad memory or idea I can pull from

Just to feel it again to help me create something worth reading, it's a
lost art, poetry
Mostly dark or have descriptive deeper meaning than meets the eye

But I hope you can't guess it correctly and appeal to my vulnerabil-
ity. That would embarrass the hell out of me, but I guess I'd be
honored

I actually have to coax myself into not using such heavy words
because I don't want to offend
My playlist has probably played five times and without me even hear-
ing the songs just over and over—The Fray, Green Day, all the
way to Taylor Swift
I don't know why I torture my eyes to this page every night
No wonder I need glasses
I can't believe it's 5:00 a.m.

November 24th

Missing you comes in waves
I often picture your beautiful face
I find myself picking up my phone to call you
Even though I know there'll be no answer
You were so proud of your grandkids and couldn't wait to show them off
Your blue eyes had a sparkle only you could pull off
You taught me that inner beauty is far better than what's sold on the
    shelves
Your laugh was contagious. I knew it so well
I'll never forget our memories each one I hold close to my heart
I never thought November would rip me apart
We had a special bond and I'm thankful for the times that we shared
From watching tv shows to you brushing my hair
You were so strong and courageous and you loved the color blue
Nothing in life will ever be the same without you
So many more photos you should have been in
Nevada will never feel the same way again
Grandma Linda, I love you and I know you knew that
If I had only one wish I'd wish for you to come back

Butterfly Tattoos

The two with tattoos of a delicate beast fluttering next to one another
Sweeping beside them like the deep seas kissing at their feet
Smashing and crashing alike the tide, the two vastly different girls
    were meant to collide
With etchings on their skin, they had no clue where to begin

Bonding over the separate trauma of their pasts, they compared scars
    of abnegation at last
As the scars they endured began to hide beneath the dye, they began
    to wonder why life was being so unfair
Taking so much and giving so little, all they knew was how to be
    belittled
To take on the pain and endure the abuse, there wasn't a use to fight-
    ing the truth

Looking for some form of comfort, they found the cursed leather
    chair, with ink dividing their skin, they were ready to sin
The pain of the needles pressure exciting the bloodlust running
    through their veins, striving to feel it again
They were both addicted to the cut

Prancing to the beat of similar drums with contrasting lyrics—one
    dark as night, the other light as day
But they don't always appear as they seem

Raven locks battling with rocks, as the paper-haired girl let them
    squash her with the lighthearted portrayal came the darkly derail
As the badass temptress was angelic to the touch with a simple "I
    don't care" her frail heart is crushed.
Divinity of both the angel hidden in the devil's wings, the two came
    together to make their silhouettes sing

Tantalizing anger and tickling defeat, laughing at the harsh air sur-
rounding the dark leather seat
Combining the havoc of their smiles grew while the paint imbedded
in their skin holding the only exception of forever in a pen
Bonding them together for life at last, they have the same beastly
wings to match

Vault

Do you ever want to just rip out your hair?
She's copying me and acts without a care
I had enough so I shut her out
If there were a lock, she'd pick it, no doubt
The girl who I once felt the most competition
Would soon hold me close as I cried in the kitchen
I saw her as a threat or a ruthless enemy
I didn't realize she actually looked up to me

Do you ever want to piss someone off
For a little competition to see if you fought
What she didn't know was I loved her more than words
With all my little antics Hate was all she heard
I pinned magazines on the wall like her to show her I'm cool
I never abided by any of her rules
I lost her for a while due to my lack of empathy
Never able to show her how much she meant to me
Though one night in her old SUV
We laughed till our cheeks turned reddish pink
We started to cry then held each other for a while
I finally was the reason for her beautiful smile

CPSIA information can be obtained
at www.ICGtesting.com
Printed in the USA
LVHW030449301121
704812LV00002B/224